Beneath the Depth of Redemption

Jonah's Journey – Translation and Exegesis

Rabbi Shaul Ben Danyiel

ISBN: 979-8-9909387-0-0 (Paperback)

Lion's Den Publications LLC
LionsDen.info

YouTube: @rabbishaulb.danyiel3830
Tiktok: @rabbidanyiel

DEDICATION

This book is dedicated to all those who have had faith in my potential as a spiritual leader and have listened to me when I taught from scripture or language. It is also dedicated to my greatest fans: my lovely wife, Devorah; my three sons, Yechezkiel BarShaul, Israel Aharon, and Adam Betzalel; and my daughter, Mia Atarah.

CONTENTS

ACKNOWLEDGMENTS

This year has been a challenge for me. I have a whole pipeline of books to write. I have collected several ideas and developed some of those ideas. However, as I must work full-time to take care of my family, I have had to put my thoughts and ideas for books on hold. Until this year, when I took a leap of faith as a man of faith and left my secure Government job as an Accountant, where I was auditing defense contracts—a job that has been a steady source of income and support for my family. I took a leap of faith and started to go on multiple short missions with my Army Reserve position to allow me time to focus on writing during these short deployments. Therefore, first and foremost, I always want to thank the Almighty because the Almighty has and will always take care of us.

Second, I want to thank my family, specifically my wife, who supports me in my spiritual calling as a chaplain for the Army and as a Rabbi in general. This support has also allowed me to work on my calling to write works on theological and scriptural topics. I also thank my children because they are a great help and sources of pride and joy for me.

I would also like to acknowledge my colleagues in the Army Chaplain Corps. They are always a group of great individuals who always have the welfare of the soldiers in mind. All my long discussions with many Chaplains have helped me refine the ideas I need to write for books.

Specifically, for this book, I would like to thank Chaplain Candidate Dickson, who took the time to proofread my commentary. His valuable insights and feedback were pivotal in making sure that I was as clear as I could possibly be in writing this book. As we worked together during the summer of 2023 at the ROTC Summer Cadet Training, our conversations helped me clarify my ideas.

I extend my gratitude to Dr. Mykael Woodward Fisher, a great person whom I have known for close to thirty years, since before I ever became a Rabbi. He helped give this book a wonderful presentation, particularly with the artwork for the cover. May he be blessed and be able to create many more graphic art projects.

I would also like to thank my close friends who have read the manuscript and encouraged me in its publication.

FORWARD

As a religious leader, I am often asked many questions. One of the most important questions to me is: what is the best translation of scripture? I have a unique perspective on this answer since I am a linguist who speaks five languages somewhat fluently, including English as my native language, Spanish as a second household language, Hebrew as my religious language in which I pray, and Arabic, which I learned as a military voice interceptor (linguist). One of the earliest languages I learned besides English was German, which I studied in high school. Therefore, from personal experience, I can say that translations are highly biased. We bring many different things into our translations. A lot of culture is wrapped up in the language itself, making translating from one language to another very challenging. Translators are often faced with choices they must make, especially when there is a significant gap between languages. For example, English and Spanish have a gap of about one, whereas the gap between English and Arabic is about four. That is a substantial gap, indicating there are few similarities between those two languages. If this is the case, what is the gap between English and Hebrew? The gap between English and Hebrew is roughly three. I take great care in my translations and in my exegesis. (See Postscript)

Exegesis is a process where we delve into the Hebrew language, examining the words, their etymology, and their context. In Hebrew, everything stems from a three-letter root, so we compare these roots with other words. I had a personal revelation while translating the book of Jonah and working on my exegesis of the key words that stood out to me. I ran my English translation of the book of Jonah through an AI system. The bulk of the translation was accurate in Spanish. However, those particular words I wanted to emphasize through exegesis, or as we say in Hebrew, Drash, were lost in translation. I was unable to convey the same message. This led me to a new question: When we study the exegetical works of famous scholars from the past, are we missing some of the points they are trying to make?

The great Rabbi Rashi is one of the foremost Hebraic scholars of all time, with a profound understanding of both French and Hebrew. However, when we read him in English, we are not reading something directly translated from Hebrew to English but rather from French to English. While

French and English share many similarities, there are still significant differences. After all, French is a Romance language derived from ancient Latin, whereas English, at its foundation, is a Germanic language, sharing more philosophical language similarities with Germanic languages.

To have a deeper understanding, it is very important to learn Hebrew and become proficient in Biblical Hebrew. The reality is that most people do not have the ability, time, desire, or resources to become fluent in Biblical Hebrew. So the next best thing is to read in their native languages. There is a caveat: they should know that there could be translation biases in any version of scriptures that they read.

My rendering of Jonah is not meant to be a replacement for the original text. It is not meant to be authoritative either. It is only a translation that highlights the gems of thought that stand out to me as I read it in the original language of Hebrew. Although I am an Orthodox Rabbi, this is also by no means authoritative for the Jewish faith. This is why I did not include the opinions of all the giants of Judaic thought. Many of the points that I highlight might have been pointed out by others who came before me. Through my studies, I may have stumbled upon certain concepts that others might have already explained better than I could, without my knowledge. The vast depth of Hebrew studies simply means that I might not have encountered what was previously discovered. Many times, I have come to conclusions only to find that a sage of the past has already elucidated them to the world. Therefore, any lack of recognition towards previous ideas is completely unintentional.

Enjoy the deep dive that I took into the Hebrew language of the story of Jonah. May it be a story that can touch you and elevate your understanding of the process of redemption.

Note: Other references to scripture that are not from the book of Jonah are from the Stone Edition

Tanach.

INTRODUCTION

The word HaShem appears throughout the book since this word literally means "The Name" and refers to the unpronounceable four-letter Divine name, Y-H-V-H (יהוה). Some say it is an acronym for the Hebrew Yehey-Haha-v'Hoveh, which means in Hebrew, "He will be, He is, and He was." It points to the eternal nature of the Almighty. As the Creator of all things in the universe, the Almighty has compassion and mercy for all peoples. The Creator is not just merciful to the chosen people. The phrase "the chosen people" is one of the most misunderstood phrases in religion, as they did nothing to be chosen of themselves. They are chosen because Our Father Abraham (Avraham Avinu) turned from idolatry, and the Almighty then chose him and his descendants to represent the Almighty to the rest of humanity. The Jewish people are not chosen to receive blessings exclusively; quite the opposite, they are chosen to share blessings with the rest of humanity. They are chosen to exemplify a holy, devout, and pious life and to demonstrate the true essence of the Torah to the world—not to proselytize but to set an example. They are chosen to be a light unto the nations, as

6

stated in Isaiah. "I am HaShem; I have called you with righteousness; I will strengthen your hand; I will protect you; I will set you for a covenant to the people, for a light to the nations;" (Isaiah 42:6).

The story of redemption is for all, and the timing of when the story is read in a Jewish synagogue is part of the story of redemption for all mankind. Jonah represents the Jewish nation to the world, and Jews are to repeat the story on the Day of Atonement every year to remind themselves that they have an obligation to the rest of humanity. A reading of Jonah is intended to remind Jews that they need to reach out to the world regardless of how the rest of the world treats them. It serves as a reminder that Jews should not act like Jonah. The Almighty loves all of creation. Read the story and share its valuable lessons with the rest of the world. These lessons of redemption emphasize the fact that the Almighty loves all of creation.

CHAPTER ONE HEBREW TEXT

אַ ויהי דבר־יהוה אל־יונה בן־אמתי לאמר:

בַּ קום לך אל־נינוה העיר הגדולה וקרא עליה כי־עלתה רעתם לפני:

גַ ויקם יונה לברח תרשישה מלפני יהוה וירד יפו וימצא אניה באה תרשיש ויתן שכרה וירד בה לבוא עמהם תרשישה מלפני יהוה:

דַ ויהוה הטיל רוח־גדולה אל־הים ויהי סער־גדול בים והאניה חשבה להשבר:

הַ וייראו המלחים ויזעקו איש אל־אלהיו ויטילו את־הכלים אשר באניה אל־הים להקל מעליהם ויונה ירד אל־ירכתי הספינה וישכב וירדם:

וַ ויקרב אליו רב החבל ויאמר לו מה־לך נרדם קום קרא אל־אלהיך אולי יתעשת האלהים לנו ולא־נאבד:

זַ ויאמרו איש אל־רעהו לכו ונפילה גורלות ונדעה בשלמי הרעה הזאת לנו ויפלו גורלות ויפל הגורל על־יונה:

חַ ויאמרו אליו הגדה־נא לנו באשר למי הרעה הזאת

לנו מה־מלאכתך ומאין תבוא מה ארצך ואי־מזה עם
אתה:

ט ויאמר אליהם עברי אנכי ואת־יהוה אלהי השמים אני
ירא אשר־עשה את־הים ואת־היבשה:

י וייראו האנשים יראה גדולה ויאמרו אליו מה־זאת
עשית כי־ידעו האנשים כי־מלפני יהוה הוא ברח
כי־הגיד להם:

יא ויאמרו אליו מה־נעשה לך וישתק הים מעלינו כי
הים הולך וסער:

יב ויאמר אליהם שאוני והטילני אל־הים וישתק הים
מעליהם כי־ידעו האנשים כי־הוא ברח מלפני:

יג ויחתרו האנשים להשיב אל־היבשה ולא יכלו כי הים
הולך וסער עליהם:

יד ויקראו אל־יהוה ויאמרו אנה יהוה אל־נא נאבדה
בנפש האיש הזה ואל־תתן עלינו דם נקיא כי־אתה יהוה
כאשר חפצת עשית:

טו וישאו את־יונה ויטילהו אל־הים ויעמד הים מזעפו:

טז וייראו האנשים יראה גדולה את־יהוה ויזבחו־זבח
ליהוה וידרו נדרים:

CHAPTER ONE TRANSLATION & EXEGESIS

1:1 The word of HaShem came to Jonah son of Ammittai saying:

1:2 Arise, go to Nineveh, that great city and cry out, (Proclaim) upon it, because its evilness has ascended before Me.

1:3 Jonah rose to escape (flee) towards Tarshish away from before HaShem. He went down to Yaffo and found a ship that was headed to Tarshish. He paid the fare and boarded it to go with them towards Tarshish from before HaShem.

1:4 HaShem hurled a mighty wind to the Sea, and there was a great storm in the Sea. It was thought that the ship would shatter.

1:5 The Sailors were terrified, and each man screamed to his god. They threw out all their vessels (utensils, pots, etc), which were in the ship to the Sea to lighten the ship unto themselves. Jonah descended to the hull of the ship and laid down and fell asleep.

1:6 The Captain of the ship drew near and said to him, "What is with you that you are sleeping?" "Get up and cry out to your god, perhaps the god will come around for us and not cause us to be perished."

1:7 Each man said to his fellow, "Come, let's go and cast lots, and we will know for whom causes this evil to be upon us." Lots were cast, and the lot fell upon Jonah.

1:8 They said unto him, "Please describe for us, as to why this evil is upon us. What is your profession? From where do you come, what is your land? From what people are you?"

1:9 He said unto them, "I am a Hebrew. I fear HaShem the God of Heaven, which made the Sea and the dry land."

1:10: The men were terrified, and said unto him, "What did you do?", because the men knew that he fled from before the presence of HaShem since he told them.

1:11: They said to him, "What should we do, so that the sea will quiet down for us?" Since the sea grew tempestuous.

1:12: He said to them, "Lift me up and heave me into the sea, and the sea will quiet down for you. Since I know it is because of me that this great storm has come upon us."

1:13: The men rowed hard to return to the dry land and could not. Since the sea raged more tempestuously upon them.

1:14: They cried out to HaShem saying, "Please HaShem, please do not allow us to perish for the soul of this man. Do not hold us on innocent blood. Since you are HaShem, and you do as you desire."

1:15 They lift Jonah and heaved him into the sea. The sea ceased from its raging anger.

1:16 Then the men greatly feared HaShem. They offered a sacrifice unto HaShem and made vows.

Chapter One Exegetical Notes:

Verse 1 - Jonah ben Amittai is also mentioned in Scripture outside of the book that bears his name. He was a prophet according to II Kings 14:25, which names him specifically, and believed in Judaism to be a student of Elisha according to II Kings 9:1, although not specifically mentioned there.

The 1901 Jewish Encyclopedia states, "According to rabbinical sources (Yer. Suk. 5:55a; Gen. R.; Yalá¸³., Jonah, Â§ 550), Ammittai came from the tribe of Zebulun and lived at Zarephath. There is a tradition that the widow who sustained the prophet Elijah there (1 Kings 17:9-24) was Ammittai's wife, and that the child whom Elijah revived was Jonah (Pirá¸³e R. El.)."

The tradition holds that Jonah was then instructed under Elisha after Elijah passed the mantle of being the prophet of the day to Elisha.

Verse 2 – The word קרא (Qara) means to call out, to vocalize, to proclaim a message, to give a proclamation, to read aloud from a scroll.

Verse 3 - The word תרשישה (Tarshisha) means "toward Tarshish." This is not how you would say it in Hebrew but how you would say it in Aramaic. It is believed by many scholars that Tarshish refers to the Iberian Peninsula. It is also believed by many that the word "Iberian" has its roots in the word Ivri, which means Hebrew.

Side Note: There are teachings that under King Solomon, his empire extended to the British Isles, where tin was mined in Cornwall. One of the most famous cities where we can track the changes in the name of the city is the modern city of Cadiz. In ancient times, the Iberian people called it Gadira, then it was changed to Gades, then to Qādis, and finally to the modern city of Cadiz, where the people there are called Gaditanos. The name Gadira in the Hebrew language would mean "City of Gad," which was one of the tribes of the ancient Israelites. This is the ultimate reason he was headed to Tarshish, one of the farthest outposts of the Hebrews during his time.

The Book of Jonah
Translation and Exegesis

CHAPTER TWO HEBREW TEXT

א וימן יהוה דג גדול לבלוע את־יונה ויהי יונה במעי
הדג שלשה ימים ושלשה לילות:

ב ויתפלל יונה אל־יהוה אלהיו ממעי הדגה:

ג ויאמר קראתי מצרה לי אל־יהוה ויענני מבטן שאול
שועתי שמעת קולי:

ד ותשליכני מצולה בלבב ימים ונהר יסבבני
כל־משבריך וגליך עלי עברו:

ה ואני אמרתי נגרשתי מנגד עיניך אך אוסיף להביט
אל־היכל קדשך:

ו אפפוני מים עד־נפש תהום יסבבני סוף חבוש לראשי:

ז לקצבי הרים ירדתי הארץ ברחיה בעדי לעולם ותעל
משחת חיי יהוה אלהי:

ח בהתעטף עלי נפשי את־יהוה זכרתי ותבוא אליך
תפלתי אל־היכל קדשך:

ט משמרים הבלי־שוא חסדם יעזבו:

י ואני בקול תודה אזבחה־לך אשר נדרתי אשלמה
ישועתה ליהוה:

יא ויאמר יהוה לדג ויקא את־יונה אל־היבשה:

CHAPTER TWO TRANSLATION & EXEGESIS

2:1 HaShem appointed a sea creature to swallow Jonah. Jonah was in the innards of the fish for three days and three nights.

2:2 Jonah prayed to HaShem his God from the innards of the sea creature.

2:3 He said, "I called out from my suffering affliction unto HaShem, and HaShem answered me." "Out of the belly of the pit I cried out in a vow, and you heard my voice."

2:4 "You cast me into the depths into the heart of the sea. The river surrounded me. All the billows and waves passed over me."

2:5 I said, "I am casted out, driven out, like a divorced woman from before your eyes that was against your eyes. Yet I increase in desire to look again at the inner sanctuary of your Holy Temple."

2:6 "The waters encompass the soul; the depth surrounds me. The seaweeds were wrapped around my head."

2:7 "I descended to the bases of the mountains; the

bars of the earth enclosed around me forever; yet you lifted my life from the pit, HaShem my God.

2:8 "When my soul was enveloped within me, I remembered HaShem. My prayer came to you, into the holy place of your temple.

2:9 "Those that guard false vanities they leave behind their own mercies.

2:10 "With a voice of thanksgiving I will sacrifice to you. That which I vowed, I will fulfill. Salvation is from HaShem."

2:11 HaShem spoke to the sea creature, and it vomited out Jonah upon the dry land.

Chapter Two Exegetical Notes:

Verse 1: The words גדול דג (Dag Gadol, literally "a large fish") are commonly understood to refer to a whale-like sea creature.

Verse 2-10 is a poem, and therefore the choice of words is pivotal. Therefore, no great translation can replace the emotional nuances contained in the original Hebrew.

Verse 2: The words הדגה ממעי (Mimey haDagah) mean "the innards of the sea creature." The choice of words conveys something deep from within. Many Psalms carry a similar idea of crying out from deep within the soul, but here it is not deep within Jonah; rather, he is deep within the sea creature.

Verse 3: The words שאול מבטן (M'beten She'ol) mean "From the belly of Sheol" or "From the belly of Hell." Could it be possible that Jonah died during his encounter with the giant sea creature, and at the moment the sea creature vomited him out, the Almighty restored life to Jonah? See below in the postscript about a modern-day man who was caught up in the mouth of a whale. I envision Jonah getting trapped in the mouth of this sea creature, covered and surrounded by seaweed, and drowning. How miserable would it be for the whale to try to vomit up Jonah, whose foot was caught? In my note to chapter one, verse one, I mentioned that there is a teaching that Jonah was already revived from the dead by Elijah; this would make it a second time. Remember that for trivia night.

Verse 4: The word מצולה (M'tzulah) is translated as "depths." However, the word itself has the root צל (Tzel), which means shadow. The word "shadow" has a relationship to darkness because a shadow is darkness, but it also casts an image. The root has two letters: צ (Tzade), which by itself means righteousness, and ל (Lamed), which means teaching or instruction. Therefore, to stand in the shadow of God would mean to learn. The person credited with building the Tabernacle in the wilderness was a young man called Betzalel, whose name means "In the shadow of God." A couple of Psalms that have similar language to this passage of scripture are: 1) Psalm 42:8, "Watery deep calls out to watery deep, to the roar of your watery channels, all Your breakers and your waves have swept over me," and 2) Psalm 69:2-3, "Save me, Oh God, for the waters have reached my soul! I am sunk in the mire of the shadowy depths, and there is no foothold; I have entered watery depths, and a rushing current sweeps me away."

Verse 5: The words עיניך מנגד נגרשתי (Nigrashti m'neged einecha), "I was cast out before your eyes." These are words that are used in divorce.

The words קדשך היכל (Haykel Kadshcha), "In the temple there are three main parts: the Courtyard, the Holy Place, and the Holy of Holies." The word

Haykel is a play on words here because it also means the skeleton in Semitic languages. The normal word for the Temple is Beit HaMikdash or the Holy House. Therefore, as Jonah was looking at the skeleton of the giant sea creature that he was stuck inside, he was referencing his longing to be in the Haykel or the holy part of the Temple.

Verse 6: The words עד־נפש מים אפפוני (Afaufuni mayim ad nefesh), "The waters encompassed me, even to the soul." The statement "The waters encompass the soul" has a striking similarity to Psalm 69:1, which states, "Save me, O God! For the waters have come up to my neck."

Verse 7: The words הרים לקצבי (L'qitzvey Harim), "At the roots of the mountains." The bottoms of the ocean's mountains.

The words חיי משחת (Mishachat Chayai) mean "to wipe out my life," and that is what the passage seems to be referencing.

Verse 8: The words נפשי עלי בהתעטף (B'hita'Teyf Alay Nafshi), "My soul enveloped upon me." In the morning, when a Jewish man goes to pray, he recites a blessing before putting on the Tallit (Prayer Shawl). It is, "Blessed are you, Lord our God, who has sanctified us with His commandments, and has commanded us to envelop ourselves in the Tzitzit." Then we wrap ourselves up in the Tallit.

Verse 9: The words הבלי־שוא משמרים (M'shamrim Havley-shav), which means "guarding false vanities," could also mean guarding worthless idols.

Verse 11: The word יקא (Yaquey) means "to vomit," and at the same time, it is an onomatopoeia, the formation of a word from a sound associated with what is named. This is the sound someone makes when trying to vomit up something.

א ויהי דבר־יהוה אל־יונה שנית לאמר:

ב קום לך אל־נינוה העיר הגדולה וקרא אליה
את־הקריאה אשר אנכי דבר אליך:

ג ויקם יונה וילך אל־נינוה כדבר יהוה ונינוה היתה
עיר־גדולה לאלהים מהלך שלשת ימים:

ד יחל יונה לבוא בעיר מהלך יום אחד ויקרא ויאמר
עוד ארבעים יום ונינוה נהפכת:

ה ויאמינו אנשי נינוה באלהים ויקראו־צום
וילבשו־שקים מגדולם ועד־קטנם:

ו ויגע הדבר אל־מלך נינוה ויקם מכסאו ויעבר אדרתו
מעליו ויכס שק וישב על־האפר:

ז ויזעק ויאמר בנינוה מטעם המלך וגדליו לאמר האדם
והבהמה הבקר והצאן אל־יטעמו מאומה אל־ירעו ומים
אל־ישתו:

ח ויתכסו שקים האדם והבהמה ויקראו אל־אלהים
בחזקה וישבו איש מדרכו הרעה ומן־החמס אשר
בכפיהם:

ט מי־יודע ישוב ונחם האלהים ושב מחרון אפו ולא
נאבד:

יַ וירא האלֹהים את־מעשיהם כי־שבו מדרכם הרעה
וינחם האלהים על־הרעה אשר־דבר לעשות־להם ולֹא
עשה:

CHAPTER THREE TRANSLATION & EXEGESIS

3:1 The word of HaShem came unto Jonah the second time, saying:

3:2 Arise and go to Nineveh, that great city, and cry out to it the proclamation which I spoke unto you.

3:3 Jonah arose and went to Nineveh according to the word of HaShem. Nineveh was a great city to God, which was three days walk across.

3:4 Jonah began to come into the city a day's journey. He proclaimed and said, "Forty more days and Nineveh will be overthrown."

3:5 The people of Nineveh believed in God, and proclaimed a fast and wore sackcloth. Everyone from the greatest to the least among them.

3:6 The word arrived and touched the King of Nineveh, and he arose from his throne, and he took off his royal garments and covered himself with sackcloth, and he sat in the ashes.

3:7 He screamed and said in Nineveh; a decree of the King and his nobles; saying 'Let neither man nor beast, herd nor flock, taste anything; let them not feed, nor drink water.

3:8 but let them be covered in sackcloth, both man and beast, and cry mightily unto God. Let everyone repent from his evil ways and from the violence that is in their hands.

3:9 He who knows repents and the God will relent and will turn away from His fierce wrath and we will not perish.

3:10 God saw their works that they repented of their evil ways, and God relented about the evil, which He said He would do to them, and He did not do it.

Chapter Three Exegetical Notes:

Verse 2: את־הקריאה אליה וקרא (U'qra eleyha et ha'qre'ah) - Cry out a proclamation. אנכי is the poetic version of the personal pronoun "I." It is used in the Ten Sayings (Ten Commandments) as the pronoun God uses to reference Himself. The normal personal pronoun for "I" is אני (ani).

Verse 3: לאלהים עיר־גדולה היתה ונינוה (v'nin'veh haytah ir gadolah l'elohim) - Nineveh was a great city to God. This is a problematic passage because it says 'for God.' Why would Jonah have a problem going there? One interpretation that I have heard before is that Nineveh held significance or importance in the eyes of God. We are not told in the book of Jonah why this phrase is used. It seems counter-intuitive. Possibly the phrase reflects its significance in the eyes of God within the narrative of the book of Jonah. Another idea is that it once was a great city for God, but we really do not have evidence that it was a righteous or holy city ever.

Verse 5: They believed ויאמינו (V'ya'miynu) - the root is related to Amen. Why did they believe immediately? There are a couple of ideas. One is the appearance of Jonah as someone who survived from within the belly of a giant sea creature.

Possibly the acid from the sea creature's digestive system stripped Jonah of color, or possibly he had a body odor that he could not get rid of. It is important to note that the people of Nineveh worshipped a deity known as Dagon. Dagon was associated with water. Fish symbolism was prevalent in the ancient Near East, and fish were often associated with water deities. So they would have looked at Jonah's God as a God who could defeat Dagon. However, there is another opinion on why they were quick to turn to the message from God, and that is because, as stated in 3:3, it once was a great city for God, and knowledge of that was still among them.

Verse 6: The word ויגע (Vayiga) means to reach, touch, or have an impact. Here we see that not only did the word of God reach the King of Nineveh, but it also had a profound impact on him, causing him to immediately go into mourning and declare that all of Nineveh should do the same.

Verse 7: The word ויזעק (V'Yazeych) means to cry out in suffering, as opposed to קרא (Qara), which means to call out. It is a more powerful word to use in this context. המלך מטעם (Mitaam HaMelech) is a play on words, literally meaning "from the taste of the King" or simply "declared". טעם (Taam) means taste, and there is to be no tasting of anything during the fast.

Verse 8: הרעה (HaRa'a) means evil ways. החמס
(HeyChamas) means lawlessness or violence.
בכפיהם (B'khafeyhem) means in their hands. What
were their evil ways? The scripture goes on to tell
us that it was their lawlessness or violence. This is
the same word that is used in Genesis 6:11 in
relation to the generation that was wiped out by the
flood.

Verse 10: It is important to note here that there is no
sacrifice. A sacrifice was not requested from God,
and there is no mention of a sacrifice. Instead, God
wants the heart that asks for forgiveness. (Refer to
Hosea 6:6, Micah 6:6-8, Isaiah 1:11-17, and
Jeremiah 7:21-23.)

The Book of Jonah
Translation and Exegesis

CHAPTER FOUR HEBREW TEXT

א וירע אל-יונה רעה גדולה ויחר לו:

ב ויתפלל אל-יהוה ויאמר אנה יהוה הלוא-זה דברי
עד-היותי על-אדמתי על-כן קדמתי לברח תרשישה כי
ידעתי כי אתה אל-חנון ורחום ארך אפים ורב-חסד ונחם
על-‏ :

ג ועתה יהוה קח-נא את-נפשי ממני כי טוב מותי מחיי:

ד ויאמר יהוה ההיטב חרה לך:

ה ויצא יונה מ‎ן-העיר וישב מקדם לעיר ויעש לו שם
סכה וישב תחתיה בצל עד אשר יראה מה-יהיה בעיר:

ו וימן יהוה-אלהים קיקיון ויעל מעל ליונה להיות צל
על-ראשו להציל לו מרעתו וישמח יונה על-הקיקיון
שמחה גדולה:

ז וימן האלהים תולעת בעלות השחר למחרת ותך
את-הקיקיון וייבש:

ח יהי כזרח השמש וימן אלהים רוח קדים חרישית ותך
השמש על-ראש יונה ויתעלף וישאל את-נפשו למות
ויאמר טוב מותי מחיי:

ט ויאמר אלהים אל-יונה ההיטב חרה-לך על-הקיקיון
ויאמר היטב חרה-לי עד-מות:

31

יַ וַיאמר יהוה אתה חסת על־הקיקיון אשר לא־עמלת בו
ולא גדלתו שבן־לילה היה ובן־לילה אבד:

יא וַאני לא אחוס על־נינוה העיר הגדולה אשר יש־בה
הרבה משתים־עשרה רבו אדם אשר לא־ידע בין־ימינו
לשמאלו ובהמה רבה:

CHAPTER FOUR TRANSLATION & EXEGESIS

4:1 A great evil was on Jonah, and he was angry.

4:2 He prayed to HaShem and said, "Please HaShem, wasn't this what I said while still in my land. Therefore, I went forward to flee to Tarshish. Since I knew that you are a gracious God, compassionate, long suffering, and abundant in mercy, and relenting upon the evil.

4:3 Now HaShem, take my soul from me, since my death is better than my life."

4:4 HaShem said, "Is it good for you to be angry?"

4:5 Jonah exited the city and sat east of the city. He made a Sukkah, a temporary dwelling for himself, and sat under it in the shade, to see what would happen to the city.

4:6 HaShem appointed a gourd to grow up over Jonah that it would provide shade for his head to save him from his evil. Jonah was exceedingly glad about the gourd.

4:7 HaShem appointed a worm when the morning rose the next day, and it cut down the gourd and it withered away.

4:8 It was when the sun rose God appointed a stifling east wind, and the sun beat upon the head of Jonah, and he fainted. He requested to his soul to die, and he said, "it is better for me to die than to live."

4:9 God said to Jonah, "You are greatly angered for the gourd?" He said, "I am greatly angered to the point of death."

4:10 HaShem said, "You have pity for the Gourd, which you did not work for it or make it grow, which was there at night and lost in a night.

4:11 Should I not have pity on Nineveh, that great city, where there are more than a hundred and twenty thousand people which do not know their right hand from their left hand, and a lot of cattle?"

Chapter Four Exegetical Notes:

4:1 The word וירע (Vayera) is a verb form for evil.
It seems to be a type of agitation or displeasure.
Later in the sentence, it says גדולה רעה (Ra'ah
Gadolah), which means a great evil. There is no
word for this in English, since we do not have a
verb for evil. Here, the word is used as a verb. Both
the verb for 'evil' seem to be a poetic connection to
the phrase 'a great evil,' giving us a sense of what
happened to him; thus, a great evil was on Jonah, or
a great evil befell Jonah. In other words, to use evil
as a verb is a poetic way to emphasize it.

4:2 The phrase ורב־חסד אפים ארך ורחום אל־חנון (El
Chanun v'Rachum Erech Apayim v'Rav Chesed) is
a powerful expression meaning "merciful and
gracious God, slow to anger, and abounding in
steadfast love and faithfulness." It is found in the
book of Exodus (Shemot) 34:6, and it is the part in
the story where God reveals His attributes and
proclaims His holy name to Moses while Moses
was in the cleft of the rock. This is a powerful
recitation that is prayed during liturgical portions
about repentance and recited multiple times on the
Day of Atonement (Yom Kippur). The word נחם
(Nicham), means "to relent." However, it is a
unique word in this sentence since it is related to the
word **Nachum**, which means comfort. So it conveys

35

an idea that when God relents from punishment because of the repentant person, God then comforts the repentant person instead.4:5 The word סכה (Sukkah) is a booth, or a temporary dwelling place. It is said that the children of Israel lived in these Sukkahs while they were in the wilderness for forty years and there is a holiday of Sukkot which follows the Day of Atonement (Yom Kippur) see note for 4:2. Since both the phrase that is discussed in verse 4:2 and the word Sukkah it is believed that the story took place at the same time of the year. Thus, it is appropriate and fitting to read the book of Jonah on Yom Kippur. This is because both Yom Kippur and the story of Jonah deal with repentance.

4:6 The word צל (Tzel) means "shade" or, more precisely, "shadow." This is a shadow over his head to deliver him from his evil. If you remember, during the time in the wilderness, there was a pillar of fire by night and a cloud by day. "Who goes before you on the way to seek out for you a place for you to encamp, with fire by night to show you the road that you should travel and with a cloud by day!" (Deuteronomy 1:34). What else can it mean? The word is made with the (צ) Tzade for

"Righteousness" and (ל) Lamed for "Learning." It reminds me of the character Betzalel (בצלאל), whose name means "in the Shadow of God." Here,

36

possibly conveying an idea that as one sits in the shadow provided by God, he learns a righteous lesson like Betzalel. Now, if Jonah can sit in the shade and have some righteous learning, then this can deliver him from his evil thoughts about the people of Nineveh. Refer to my note on verse 2:4; this brings it full circle.

4:8 The word תָּךְ (Tauch) is often translated as "beat down." The sun beat down on Jonah. The word here is something akin to "strike," "smote," or "cut." In English, we would say something like "beat down on him." Here, the words carry a stronger meaning. Obviously, Jonah did not learn the lesson of verse 4:6.

4:11 The phrase לשמאלו ימינו (Yemeno l'shmolo) is about directionality. It literally means "his right to his left." In this context, it speaks about the hand. God is telling us that the people have no clue about what is good and evil, no clue that what they are doing is even wrong.

CONCLUSION

There is a day on the Jewish calendar where all the Jews come together to fast and pray for repentance. This day is Yom Kippur. It is part of a season that begins with Rosh Hashanah, the traditional Jewish New Year. Literally, the words mean "head of the year." However, unlike traditional New Year's celebrations around the world, it is not a day for getting drunk and celebrating in lewd manners. Quite the opposite, it is a day to recognize that God created everything that exists. It is a day of judgment for the entire world, whether they know it or not. The Book of Life is opened, and judgments are rendered about who will die, who will live, who will be sick in the year, who will be poor in the year, and who will be prosperous in the year. The list goes on. However, the book is not sealed. This begins a 10-day process of great introspection and repentance. On Rosh Hashanah, the blast of the Shofar (ram's horn) is heard, just as it was at Mt. Horeb. The cry from this ram's horn is meant to wake us up and draw us close to God.

At the end of Rosh Hashanah, there is a ten-day cycle called the Days of Awe. The Jewish nation is in deep reflection. Many ask for

38

forgiveness from friends and family, all in preparation for the day of Yom Kippur. Yom Kippur is the Day of Atonement, and upon this day, at the very end of the day, after 25 hours of fasting and praying, the Book of Life, as previously mentioned, is closed. The gates to the Holy throne room are closed.

Another holiday soon follows. It is the holiday of Sukkot (The Feast of Tabernacles), which seems distinctly Jewish today due to its customs. We lost the Temple when the Romans destroyed it in 70 CE by breaching the walls and setting it ablaze. At that moment, the Romans destroyed the festival where the nation of the Jews prayed for all the other nations in the world. I have heard it said before, though I don't remember the exact quote, that if they had known and understood the profound significance of the entire Jewish world praying for the nations of the world as commanded by the Almighty on the holiday of Sukkot, they would have stationed guards themselves to protect it and never let it be destroyed.

It is through this understanding of the holidays that we observe a public reading of the book of Jonah.

The book of Jonah is read on the day of

Yom Kippur because it has several references to this season, and the story is all about redemption. The story is read towards the end of the day. One might wonder why it is read at the end of the day. It is read towards the end of the day because a shift takes place towards the end of the day after the ancient Israelites prayed for themselves. Starting with the High Priest himself and everybody else in the Israelite nation, they must then go forth with that message to the rest of the world — just like Jonah was supposed to go to Nineveh. The story is emphasized so that we do not act like Jonah. Instead, we should do what we are supposed to do according to the words of Isaiah, which are to be a light unto the nations.

"I am HaShem; I have called you with righteousness; I will strengthen your hand; I will protect you; I will set you for a covenant to the people, for a light to the nations; (Isaiah 42:6)."

POSTSCRIPT

Principles for Translation and Exegesis

Since the book of Jonah is not a legal document of Judaism, I apply three principles from the "Thirteen Principles of Torah Elucidation" attributed to Rabbi Yishmael. The Thirteen Principles are used in Jewish hermeneutics to guide the interpretation of the Torah. Rabbi Yishmael was a prominent sage who lived during the Second Temple period. These principles were developed to provide a systematic approach to understanding the deeper meanings and teachings of the Torah.

The principles that I rely upon are:

1. Equivalence of Expressions, which involves drawing connections between different verses or passages that share identical words or phrases, implying a link between their meanings.
2. Learn from the Context, which involves deriving lessons based on the context in which a particular verse or phrase appears.
3. Learn from Two Scriptural Verses, which involves deriving insights by comparing two different verses from the Torah.

Additionally, I delve into and focus on the roots. Since Hebrew is a Semitic language, all the words are derived from three-letter roots. Each letter has a pictographic as well as a phonetic meaning. This means that when words share all three root letters, they are connected in meaning, and to some extent, this applies to words that also share two of the three root letters, albeit to a lesser extent.

Finally, when there are two words that do not share the same roots but have similar sounds, there is a connection created by the sounds, which prompts us to delve deeper into the connection between the two words.

Various Beliefs on the Tomb of Jonah

According to some traditions, the tomb of the biblical prophet Jonah is believed to be in Mosul, Iraq. It is situated within the Mosque of Jona (Nabi Yunus Mosque) in the city. This is not a pilgrimage spot for Jews; however, Muslims and Christians believe this is where the tomb of Jonah is located. Due to ongoing conflicts and instability in the region, it is not a place that most people can visit. Access to the site is often restricted or unsafe.

According to Jewish tradition, the tomb of Jonah, the biblical prophet, is believed to be in the town of Gath-hepher. This city is mentioned in the Book of Joshua in the Hebrew Scriptures (Joshua

19:13). Gath-hepher is in the northern part of modern-day Israel, near the city of Nazareth.

Modern Whale Phenomenon

The headline for a Jerusalem Times newspaper article dated June 13, 2021, was "Modern-Day Jonah: Cape Cod diver swallowed by humpback whale, but escapes." The article stated that "Fifty-seven-year-old commercial lobster diver Michael Packard had been diving Friday morning off Herring Cove Beach when he was suddenly swallowed into the massive maw of the giant cetacean."

The headline for a Cape Cod Times newspaper article dated June 11, 2021, was "'I was completely inside': Lobster diver swallowed by humpback whale off Provincetown." The Cape Cod Times article quoted Mr. Packard: "I could sense I was moving, and I could feel the whale squeezing with the muscles in its mouth."

ABOUT THE AUTHOR

I am a seasoned Army Chaplain who has spent over 19 years in various components of the Army. My military journey began right after graduating from high school. I joined as an Airborne Infantryman, rising to the rank of Sergeant. During the 90s, I was stationed in South Korea and later at Fort Bragg. While at Fort Bragg, I was deployed to Haiti for peacekeeping operations.

In 2000, I graduated from the Modern Standard Arabic Language Course at the prestigious Army Language School in Monterey, CA. I hold a Rabbinical Degree from Yeshiva Pirchei Shoshanim and an MBA in Global Management and Accounting. I have over two decades of accounting experience.

I have always been fascinated by the beauty of languages. Although I am a native English speaker, I embraced the Spanish language through marriage into a Spanish-speaking family. My faith tradition and Rabbinical studies have allowed me to grow in the Hebrew language. My military service equipped me to be proficient in Arabic, and I also learned German while in high school.

My proficiency in the Hebrew language has guided me in understanding spiritual truths. I have immersed myself in both Modern Semitic languages like Hebrew and Arabic, as well as Ancient Semitic Languages such as Hebrew, Aramaic, and Ugaritic.

Hebrew holds a special place in my heart as it has been a compass guiding me through the labyrinth of spiritual truths. I have a profound passion for unraveling mysteries through exegesis.

Beyond my professional pursuits, I love to travel and am eager to explore the world's tapestry of cultures. Learning foreign languages is not just a hobby; it is a lifelong quest. The study of scripture and etymology are my intellectual playgrounds.

I married an extraordinary woman from Mexico, a language scholar and instructor who shares my passion for language and travel. Together, we have three incredible sons and one wonderful daughter. They mean more to me than any of my other pursuits, and I desire to show them all the world that I have come to learn in my lifetime.

www.ingramcontent.com/pod-product-compliance
Lightning Source LLC
LaVergne TN
LVHW051807080426
835511LV00019B/3428